Table of Contents

Piecing the Blocks

This book contains all 25 blocks to make the Triangle Block Sampler Quilt. Trace the patterns to make the templates, which can be used in either hand or machine piecing. The more accurate you are when tracing your templates, the easier your blocks will fit together.

Pieced Block Templates

Freezer paper is preferred because you can easily see through it to trace the templates, and because the templates can be used several times.

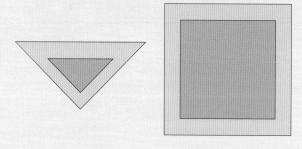

1. Place freezer paper over the drawing of the block. Trace all of the shapes onto the freezer paper; add a ¼" (6mm) seam allowance on all sides. To create exact, clear lines, use a pencil with a thin lead. Number the pieces to keep them in order.

2. Iron the freezer paper onto the right side of your fabric. Remember to set your iron to a no-steam setting.

3. Cut out all shapes and assemble them as shown on the pattern.

Foundation piecing

Foundation piecing is an easy technique to piece your blocks together. In this method, fabric is sewn to the paper foundation following a numerical sequence.

1. Decide how many units the pattern will be divided into.

2. Trace the pattern onto the foundation paper; use a ruler and thin-lead pencil. Copy all of the lines of each unit and add a ¼" (6mm) seam allowance around each unit.

3. Number the foundation paper in the order that the pieces should be sewn together. The more blocks you finish, the easier this will become.

4. Position the fabrics right sides together on the unmarked side of the foundation.

5. Stitch on the sewing line between the numbers using a very small stitch; 1.5 will work on most machines.

6. Continue stitching all of the pieces in numeric order until the block or unit is completed. Trim the fabric so that it is even with the outside line of the foundation. If you have more than one unit for a block, match the units and stitch them together.

7. Keep the foundation paper in place for now; it will help to stabilize the blocks when you sew them together with the sashing.

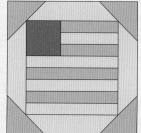

Some blocks can be pieced together as a whole unit.

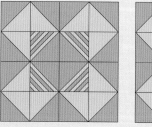
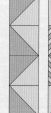
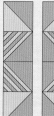
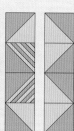

Some blocks need to be pieced together in separate units and then stitched together to make a whole unit.

Materials & Assembly

Quilt size: 54" × 54" (137cm × 137cm)
Finished Block Size: 6" × 6" (15cm × 15cm)

FABRIC

All measurements based on 44"-wide (112cm) fabric.

2 yds. (183cm) floral or geometric print with at least four colors for borders and binding.

¾ yds. (69cm) of each of the four main colors for blocks (tiny prints, tone-on-tones and solids).

2½ yds. (229cm) white or cream fabric for sashing, borders and blocks.

BACKING:

3½ yds. (320cm) coordinating 44"-wide (112cm) fabric for backing (or 1¾ yds. [160cm] 60"-wide (152.5cm) wide backing).

Batting: Twin Size

CUTTING INSTRUCTIONS

FROM THE WHITE OR CREAM FABRIC:

A - Six 2½" × 42" (6.5cm × 106.5cm) strips for vertical sashing and side borders.
B - Two 2½" × 46" (6.5cm × 117cm) strips for top and bottom borders.
C - Twenty 2½" × 6½" (6.5cm × 16.5cm) strips for sashing.

FROM THE OUTER BORDER FABRIC:

D - Two 5½" × 55" (14cm × 139.5cm) strips.
E - Two 5½" × 48" (14cm × 122cm) strips.

Note: Before piecing your blocks, plan out the color combinations for each block by labeling them. This will help with the distribution of color among the blocks, and it will be helpful in achieving a balanced composition when arranging the blocks for the quilt top. For this pattern there are twenty-five blocks total: five across and five down.

ASSEMBLING THE QUILT TOP

1. Make twenty-five blocks using the instructions on page 3 or follow your favorite piecing method.

2. Sew blocks together to create vertical rows using (C) 2½" × 6½" (6.5cm × 16.5cm) sashing strips between the blocks. Press strips toward the sashing

3. Beginning with a (A) 2½" × 42" (6.5cm × 106.5cm) sashing strip, sew the rows together. Trim the sashing pieces so they're even with the blocks.

BORDERS

After all blocks are assembled, add borders as instructed below.

WHITE/CREAM BORDERS:

1. Add the side borders with the last (A) 2½" × 42" (6.5cm × 106.5cm) sashing pieces.

2. Add the top and bottom borders with the (B) 2½" × 46" (6.5cm × 117cm) white/cream strips. Trim excess and press.

PRINTED BORDERS:

1. Add the side border (E) 5½" × 48" (14cm × 122cm) strips. Press the seam toward the raw edge and trim excess.

2. Add the top and bottom border (D) 5½" × 55" (14cm × 139.5cm) strips. Press the seam toward the border piece and trim excess.

Note: When lining up the sashing to create columns that are even and match up, mark cornerstones before piecing the sashing to the next row.

Baste the batting and backing; quilt and bind.

The Blocks

FLOWER GARDEN

DECISIONS

GOLDFISH

BLACK TIE

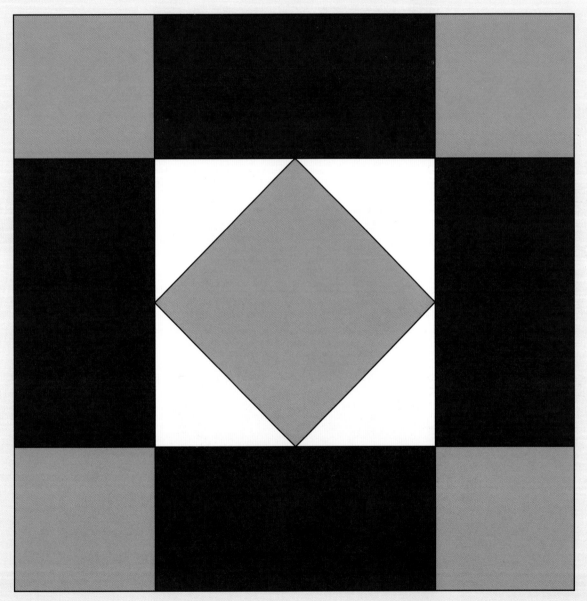

TEAM COLORS

GARDENING

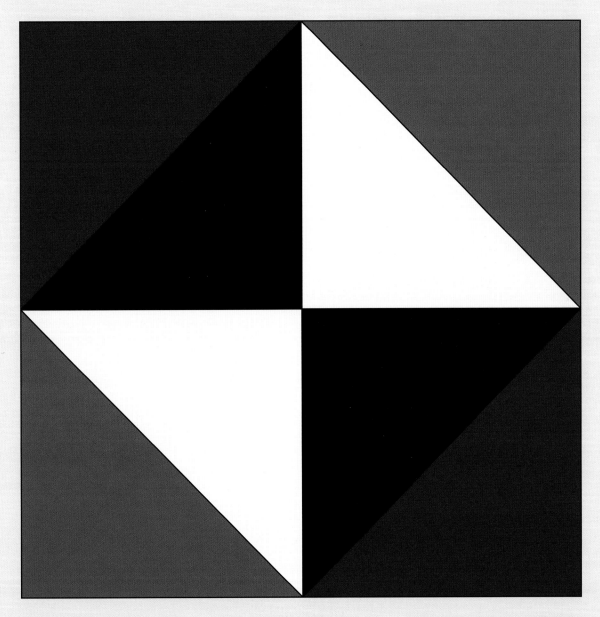

SPINNING TOP

SPOTLIGHTS

14

ADVENTURE

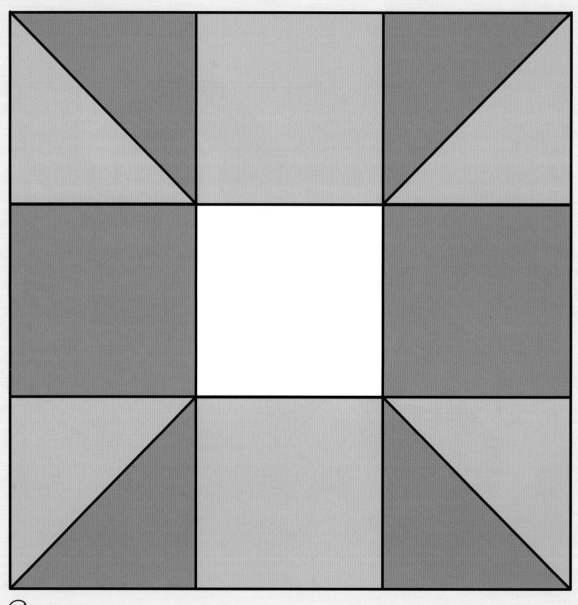

GIFTS

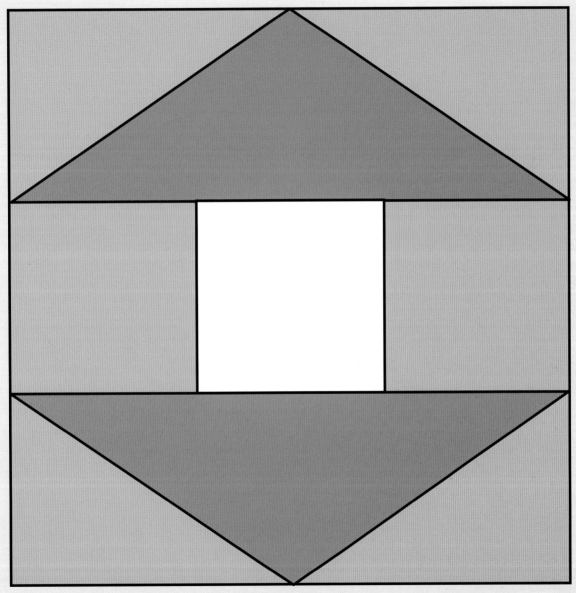

GUIDANCE

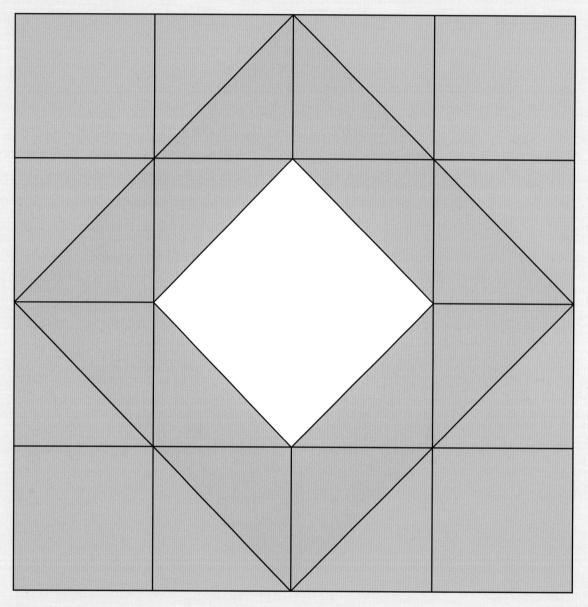

MARKET

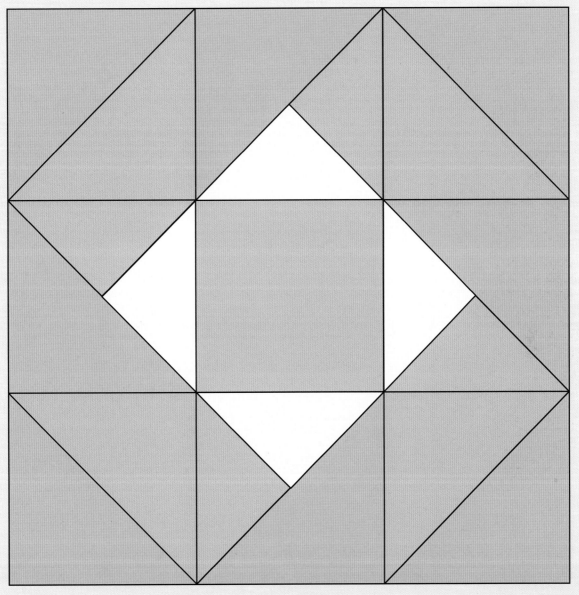

TWIRL

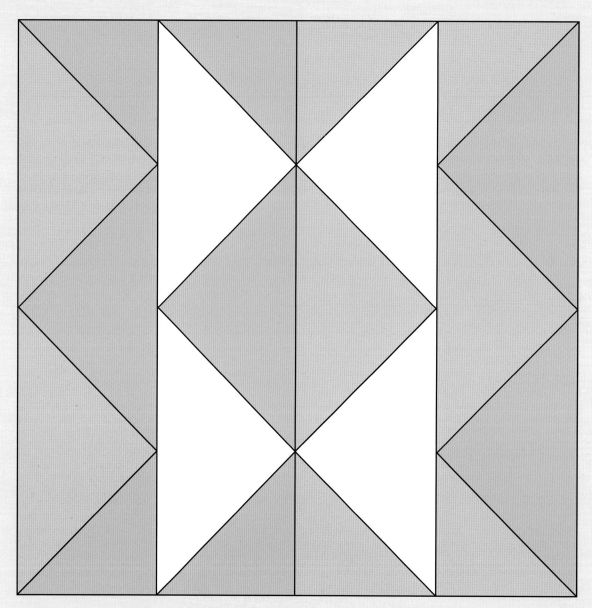

WIND & WAVES

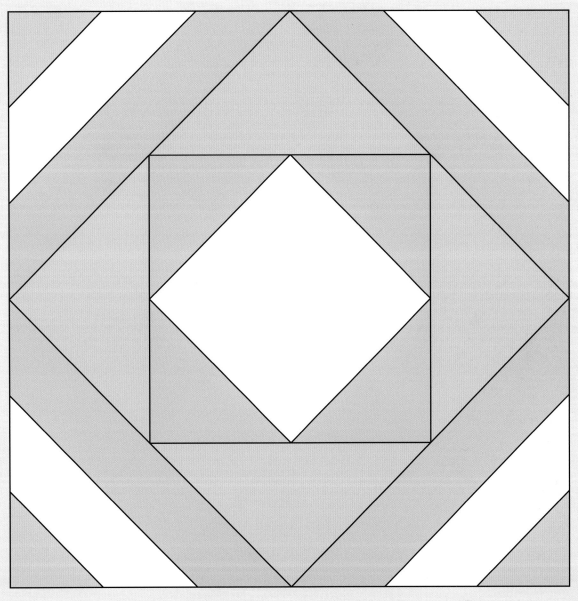

COMPASS

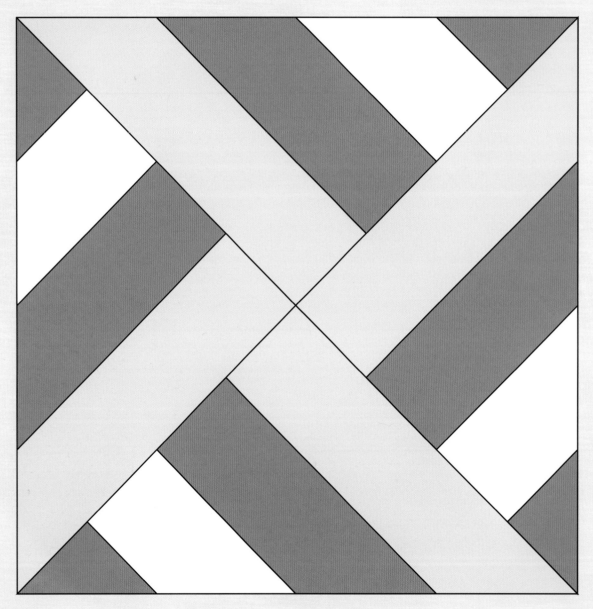

HIDDEN SURPRISE

MORNING VIEW

RISK TAKING

COLLAGE

HOURGLASS

CHOCOLATE CHIPS

RUNWAY

NATIVE

29

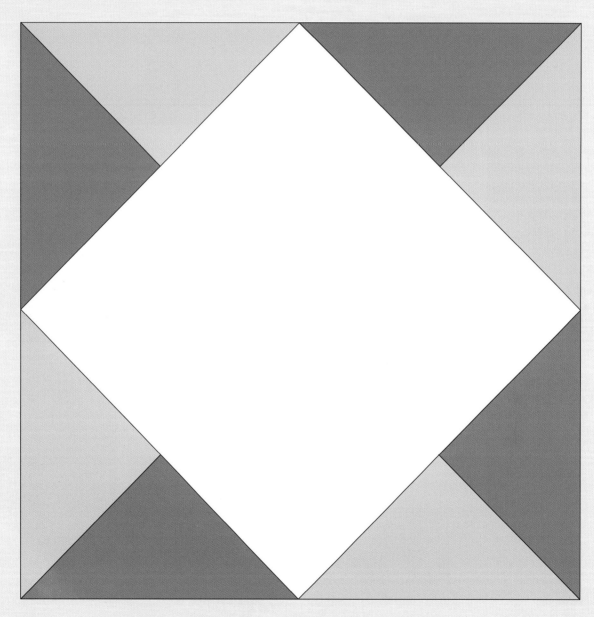

LOOKING GLASS

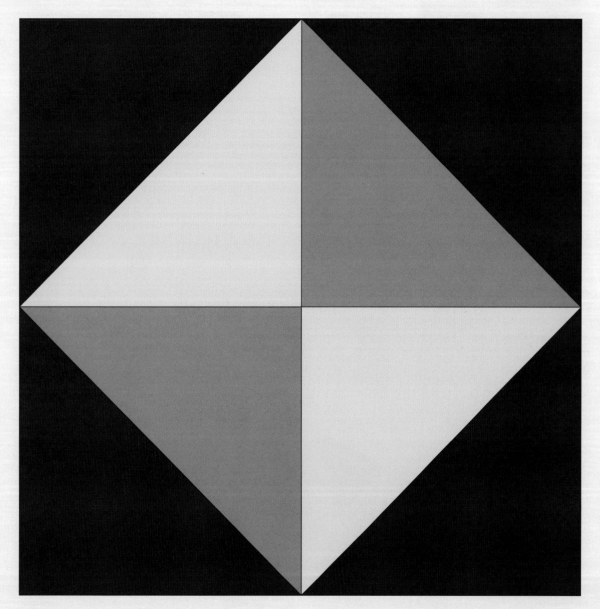

FINGER TRAP